# One
# Christmas
# I Met
# an
# Angel

# One Christmas I Met an Angel

## J. Grant Swank

Beacon Hill Press of Kansas City
Kansas City, Missouri

Copyright 1996
by Beacon Hill Press of Kansas City

ISBN 083-411-5786

Printed in the
United States of America

Cover Design: Mike Walsh

Library of Congress Cataloging-in-Publication Data

Swank, J. Grant (Joseph Grant), 1939-
   One Christmas I met an angel / J. Grant Swank, Jr.
     p.   cm.
   ISBN 0-8341-1578-6 (pbk.)
   1. Christmas—Miscellanea.   2. Jesus Christ—Nativity—Miscellanea.   3. Swank, J. Grant (Joseph Grant), 1939-
I. Title.
BV45.S945   1996
263'.91—dc20
                      96-14862
                      CIP

10   9   8   7   6   5   4   3   2   1

To my parents,
Grant and Muriel Swank

# Contents

# *Foreword*

*Christmas*—the very word floods the imagination and stirs the emotions. God chose the tiny Judean village of Bethlehem, annually revered in churches and homes around the world, as the cradle of celestial joy, hope, and peace. Each Christmas people young and old contemplate the reality and significance of the manger, the shepherds, the magi, and the holy family under the star of Bethlehem. In this hamlet one quiet, mysterious night an event took place that forever changed the course of history.

J. Grant Swank's compelling work serves as a timely reminder of the distinctive essence and implications of Christmas. He has given us something far more than delightful anecdotal vignettes. Indeed, his book genuinely captures the soul and spirit of this sacred season.

Sit back, relax, and enjoy these refreshing glimpses of Christmas through the heart and experience of one who has given his life to the Christ child's mission and ministry. *One Christmas I Met an Angel* is a treasure of inspiration and insights that belongs on the bookshelf of every pastor and in every Christian home.

The spirit and focus of this book are unapologetically Christ-centered. It contains a rare and thoroughly refreshing blend of contemporary allegories, biblical insights, and practical ideas, all of which enrich the celebration of Jesus' birthday. It also continues the fulfillment of Christ's promise—"When I am lifted up from the earth, [I] will draw all men to myself" (John 12:32, NIV).

—LT. COLONEL WILLIAM W. FRANCIS
*The Salvation Army*

# One
# Christmas
# I Met
# an
# Angel

1

# One Christmas
# I Met an Angel

*I*T WAS THE MOST DEPRESSING CHRISTMAS OF MY LIFE.

My wife and I had been married for nine years. Since our second year together, she had been ill. Now she was facing brain surgery.

Her illness forced me to leave my Midwest pastorate. We moved to my in-laws' home in New England. Medical tests followed. Then the day of surgery.

It was Christmas, but it didn't seem like Christmas to me. Traditional lights were glistening everywhere, and churches were abuzz with excitement, but I felt a coldness in my heart akin to the freezing rains that hit me as I trudged uphill to the hospital.

A world-respected physician, James L. Poppen of New England Baptist Hospital in Boston, believed the operation would relieve my wife's constant head pain. He would place a shunt in her head, connecting the brain to the heart for the release of pressure under her skull.

I spent many hours in the hospital's chapel. I basked in the quietness there as I sought God's peace for my troubled soul.

Our only daughter was in Connecticut with her grandparents while my wife and I endured that somber holiday. I could hardly believe this usually cheerful season of the year could turn so dismal.

The hospital is located atop a city hill. To get there one must climb a narrow street often treacherous with

December's ice. I drove up that tiny passage each day to be near my wife. Our Christmas Day would be spent in an old section of the hospital, with its barren walls and eerie alcoves.

I had no place to stay at night and couldn't afford a hotel. An older, unmarried friend of ours lived in a suburb nearby. Knowing that Priscilla, my wife, would be undergoing surgery and that I would be stranded in a strange city, Marian offered her home as a refuge for me during this difficult time.

During the day, Marian worked as secretary to the dean of students at a college in the area. After arriving home in the evenings, she would wait up for me like a mother hen. Upon my return from a draining day of being with my wife at the hospital, Marian would share her genuine laughter and a cup of hot tea. I needed both.

One night as I left the hospital, I discovered one of my tires was flat. My car was parked on the top of the lonely hill. My feet and hands were freezing in the awful winds.

After changing the tire, I was in no mood for celebrating any holiday, let alone the most meaningful one of the year. I was anxious to ditch it all and get on with a new year, praying that it would be a lot better than the one we had just staggered through.

When I arrived at Marian's home, I discovered that she was in a festive mood. The tiny apartment was lighted throughout. Simple refreshments were waiting on the small table, and her heart was merry.

I thanked God for the pull-out couch that was awaiting me in the den. And I was particularly grateful for this warm abode where I could dry out my dampened spirit.

"Marian, you need some practical additions to this place," I said one evening while taking stock of her living quarters. I noticed that there were a number of items missing from her kitchen—tools, baskets, racks for this and that.

"Oh, I know—and I could have bought them a long time ago, but I guess I never got around to it," she replied.

I knew Marian gave a lot of her money to college students in need. One by one she would invite them over to feed them, listen to them, and pray with them. Over the years she became so popular with the students that they set aside a special day one year and named it after her. They made her the guest of honor in that day's chapel service, presenting her with a gift from the whole student body.

Considering the typical needs of college students, I could figure out why Marian was missing one convenient device after another. So when returning one night from the hospital, I decided the Lord was nudging me to pack a collection of household gadgets into a large plastic clothes carrier.

I must have looked strange walking into that apartment building with this array of items. Nevertheless, I had more of a Christmas feeling as I climbed the several flights of stairs to her door on the top floor.

I knocked. She opened the door, and I rushed in with my assortment of gifts. One by one I lifted them into the air for her to see.

She smiled as she handled each present with delight. I darted into one space after another, suggesting just where she could use each present. Soon the kitchen and living room were adorned with new objects that spelled my thanksgiving at Christmastime.

My wife's surgery was over. There was a long recuperation period to go through. It would be well into January before she could be released from the hospital for a return trip to Connecticut.

Yet in the midst of it all, I felt that the awful loneliness of the city was beginning to ebb for both of us. We were being buoyed with new hope for the future.

"But why did you buy all these things?" Marian asked. "You can't afford these."

She was right, of course. But I could not afford to have done otherwise. I knew that without her hospitality to me at Christmas, I wouldn't have made it.

"Marian, it's the least I can do for you. You've been so kind to me that I just felt I had to do something to say thanks. So this is it."

She broke into laughter and walked toward the teapot again, ready to pour me a cup. I saw tears in her eyes as she moved into the kitchen. I knew she understood my feelings better than I could express them in words. After all, I was one of those young persons she had helped through the years.

As I sipped the steaming tea, I looked at her, framed against the Christmas lights shining from the living room window. The glow was unmistakable. It was then that I knew it to be true—in the midst of my confusion and heartache, God had sent me an angel at Christmastime.

No Christmas can ever be too bleak for Him. His messengers are still at work, no matter how dark the times.

# *All Is Bright*

THE CHRISTMAS WREATHS STILL HUNG ON THE WALLS OF THE front meeting room, but it was evident that the season's mirth had ebbed away.

Some of us from the church had gone to bring Christmas's good cheer to the convalescent home. Since other organizations had clogged the home's December calendar, we had moved our usual time to the first Sunday in January.

"Even though Christmas is over, we can still sing the carols," someone suggested. The rest of us agreed. So with songbooks in hand, we greeted our elderly friends.

One woman was not very attentive. She kept pushing the tablecloth over the table's edge, while another resident yanked at it from another direction. Neither seemed to understand what she was doing.

Across from those two was a woman who had been strapped to her chair so she would not fall onto the floor. She kept leaning forward as if to test the strength of the cloth straps. As we sang she mumbled under her breath, evidently not at all happy to be confined.

More women than men lived in the nursing home, so when two men attended services, we were pleased. But one of the men here this day had folded his arms in defiance, shouldering himself against our presence.

*This is a pitiful sight,* I thought as one of our group members read aloud from Luke 2. I wondered what the children in our group were thinking as they pondered the forlorn mood of the room. Certainly this was a far cry from what they had enjoyed in their own homes during the Christmas season.

"HOLIDAY GREETINGS" still hung in huge red-and-white letters from the beams of the ceiling. At least the banner was doing its job. It told me that someone had thought enough of the Christmas season to try to convey a hint of joy.

But how secular it all was! Even on the shelves there were only Santa figurines—not a hint of the Nativity scene. Yet surely a number of these elderly folk had church backgrounds and had at one time worshiped faithfully somewhere.

To my right there was a resident who kept shouting gibberish while we were singing "Hark! the Herald Angels Sing." The church people courteously ignored her clamor, concentrating instead on the traditional Christmas strains of gladness.

I decided the staff was to be commended for taking care of these people day in and day out. *I wonder if we're making any impact on these residents' tethered minds,* I thought.

"Let's give it our best!" I encouraged the small assembly as I announced that "Joy to the World" would be our next carol. That raised the decibels a little, but not much. Did our being here make any difference?

Outside, the frosted earth gave us no warmth to encourage our faltering attempts to communicate the gospel. Several times our group was interrupted by people who had come to the home to visit a relative or friend. As they traipsed through, they cut into what little attention we had commanded.

*Some days are like this,* I whispered to my soul. *Just keep on keeping on,* I told myself. *Be "patient in well-doing."*

One of the church women had brought along a large box of fresh oranges. It was now time for the boys and girls to hand a couple of oranges to each of the residents in attendance. As the children wove between the wheelchairs and the tables and then returned to their own seats, I watched their young faces. They wore smiles that reached up into the older ones' eyes. Their little, smooth hands touched the old, wrinkled ones.

One elderly woman took hold of the arm of a little girl and drew her near. No doubt it had been months since she had touched a child.

"The children do make a difference," I said between verses of the carol. Several nodded in agreement.

Finally it was time to pray. But it was difficult to hear the prayers, because some of the residents kept breaking in with their gibberish. Such a pity!

These people were once babies and then toddlers. They once romped as boys and girls, sliding down slopes and climbing apple trees. They had fallen in love, married, and borne children of their own. They had held jobs, paid bills, and worried about world events. But now they were lined up in a front room, hardly knowing what was going on, oblivious to the Christmas tree lights that kept blinking off and on, oblivious to it all.

"Now we're going to close with probably the favorite Christmas carol of all—let's all sing 'Silent Night.'"

A sigh seemed to breathe gently from our group as we realized we had been faithful workers for the Lord. The battle waged against the contradictions of the season was soon to be won, or at least ended, by a benediction.

Instead, a marvel happened before our eyes. During the entire program no one from the home had sung one syllable of any carol. But now, as one, they joined in to sing the simple hymn. Slowly but surely the minds came together, alert and touched by some spell from without.

"Silent night! Holy night . . ."

Lips that had seemed glued shut were now moving, singing with gladness. They *did* know why we had come. They *were* discerning the meaning of Christmas joy for one more year. That especially familiar carol had unlocked their awareness.

The two women stopped pushing and pulling at the tablecloth. The other one quit straining at her straps. The man unfolded his stiff arms. One by one the elderly were coming together with us. By the time we sang the last verse, the whole mood had changed. As the tree lights, our hearts were now also aglow.

*It has been worth it after all,* I thought. God had honored our being there. His Spirit had reached into the gloomy hearts of those too-often-forgotten ones.

"You have sung that hymn so well that I think we should sing it again as a prayer to the Christ child," I said. With that, the voices reached the ceiling as one smiling face responded to another. A wreath of cheer had come down upon all.

As I closed with prayer, I could think of no other words as appropriate as those from the carol—"all is bright." By a miracle of grace, His glory had embraced us and the season once again.

# *Christmas Means Seeing Jesus*

*E*VERY DAY IS CHRISTMAS IF ONE SEES JESUS. IT'S ALL IN SEE-ing Him.

No wonder Jesus said of himself, "I am the light of the world" (John 8:12). Without Him, all else is darkness.

One Sunday evening, while seated in church listening to the choir's rendition of a lovely Christmas cantata, I noticed one of the sopranos in the front row. This young lady spent most of the time trying to adjust the wick on an artificial candle that evidently wasn't connected with the battery and therefore wouldn't light.

She twisted and turned that tiny stub, then stroked it in hopes that a gentler touch would be more persuasive. I thought that in time she would give up, simply cup her hand over the tip of the candle, and pretend that all was well, but she never did. To the very end of the concert she kept poking at that little white stick.

As I left the building I felt sorry for the young lady. She was there the entire evening, had sung in the choir, but had missed the wonder of Christmas. *She had not seen Jesus.* All she had noticed was a defective flashlight.

In the second row of the same choir had been a middle-aged woman whose face was aglow. She was caught up with the beauty of the music and the message. I thought about the contrast between the two and concluded that the second woman was truly singing for Jesus, for her eyes were upon Him while participating in the evening's celebration.

No wonder the shepherds left Bethlehem praising and glorifying God! They had seen *Jesus.*

How was this so? Partly because they never doubted the message told them by the angels. They believed the unbelievable—that a peasant baby wrapped in swaddling clothes, laid in a cow's trough, and overseen by youthful parents was indeed the Messiah, the Son of God, the coming King. So strong was their faith that they dared to leave the barn and broadcast the exciting news to the world.

In a world of nuclear weapons, abuse of all sorts, and the disintegration of society, are we able to believe with a faith so simple that we can see Jesus? For those who will look into the manger with believing hearts, Jesus will surely be seen.

I have a friend with multiple sclerosis who is confined to a health-care center. Her husband has deserted her and is now an alcoholic. She has no children, and her parents are no longer living. The other night she phoned to say that her closest "friend"—with whom she shared a bank account—had taken her checkbook. "You don't need the money," this so-called friend had told the handicapped woman. And if that wasn't enough, the social worker in charge of her case had turned on her and was not only unpleasant but just plain nasty. "I don't know how much more I can take," my unfortunate friend told me in tears as she bared her heart over the phone.

This lady is a believer and faithfully serves the Lord in spite of her disability. Although crushed by her friend's betrayal, she took the dilemma to God in prayer.

A week later she called my home again. "I have all my money back," she said, "and the social worker has been fired from the center because of excessive drinking." Her voice broke as she quietly sobbed. There was no need to say any more. Through the darkness of her despair she had found Jesus.

To see Jesus, the shepherds did something else many people refuse to do. They were willing to kneel.

To truly see inside the manger, we must kneel; we must bend in adoration. For a person who is reaching for status and trying to climb the ladder of worldly success, kneeling is not easy. But when we are in love with the Baby—the Christ child—we bow before Him.

During a cantata there were a number of tableaus to illustrate visually the message that was being sung. I watched the children gather around the manger scene by the tree. Their faces were glowing and their eyes were shining, because lying in that crib was a baby. Kneeling, they were able to see the baby. No wonder Jesus admonished adults that if they were to be a part of His kingdom, they must become as little children.

This season, follow God's directive. Just as the shepherds were told by the angels to go and were helped in their quest with signs to keep them on track—the city of David, a Baby in swaddling clothes, a manger—so we, too, must go. When we are obedient to God, we will surely find Him.

Some people try to find God in their own way: through drugs, gurus, "trips," the occult, "psychic tickles," and "soul massages" of one sort or another. But these are *not* the means by which God has directed us to find Him.

When told by the angels to go to Bethlehem, the shepherds could have refused. They may have preferred to stay with their flocks or decided to go to Galilee instead of Bethlehem. They could have chosen dozens of other options. But they didn't. Instead, they followed God's leading. As a result, they found Jesus!

We can see Him today, even in our confused, sinful world with all that is going on to point us in the wrong direction. Listen to the angels—*do as they say.*

A few years ago a serious gas leak in India killed more than 2,500 persons. Mother Teresa never flinched but flew right into the horror. Gathered around her were swelling crowds. She turned and faced them, knowing that carcasses were being lifted from the ground to be burned in piles in the surrounding acreage.

She shared with the crowds that a beautiful thing was happening in spite of all the pain and sorrow—the tragedy was bringing out the best in everybody. It was forcing those who would otherwise never become involved to serve the suffering. Love was overcoming suffering.

Meeting with 14,000 schoolchildren, Mother Teresa urged them not to have bitter feelings. She told them that this could have been an accident. Like a fire, it could have broken out anywhere. She pointed out that it consequently was important to forgive. Forgiveness offers a clean heart, and people are a hundred times better for doing it.

It is still possible today for people of faith to bend before the manger and see Jesus.

# *Calamity at Christmas*

**W**HAT A HANDSOME TREE WE HAD BOUGHT AT THE COUNTY agricultural school! It stood tall in the corner of our living room. The stand was full of water, and all we needed to do was string the lights and hang the ornaments.

My wife traditionally places the lighted angel atop the tree. Next she carefully strings the lights from right to left all the way down the tree. The rest of us hang the decorations on the limbs.

This year we had everything in place when suddenly the tree fell over. Our older daughter was caught beneath it all. Lights went helter-skelter. Ornaments flew across the room. Water poured out of the stand, soaking into the carpet. A forlorn angel lay on its side beneath the branches. What a mess for a December Saturday afternoon!

It was not with the best of moods that we hoisted the tree upright again. We moved it to another corner so the carpet could dry out. Once more we filled the stand with water. We straightened the angel atop the tree, strung the lights, and laced the branches with decorations.

To help lift our irritated spirits, we played traditional carols throughout the house, filling the rooms with melody. Someone made a fresh pot of tea. Someone else discovered cookies in the kitchen cupboard.

Soon the front doorbell rang. Jay, our son, opened the door to find a neighbor standing there.

"Is your father home?" he asked. Jay invited him inside. I greeted my neighbor, wondering what brought him to our house that day.

"Do you think I could chat with you, perhaps even have prayer?" The man looked intently into my face.

Because there was so much bustle in our house, I quickly reasoned that it would be best for the two of us to walk across to the nearby church sanctuary. I grabbed my winter jacket and the church keys as my friend followed behind me.

Once inside the church, he spilled out his woe.

"I need prayer. My family needs prayer. I knew when I passed your church sign that God told me to stop and ask for you to pray with me."

I was curious about what was bothering this young man. Often we had waved to each other in passing. From time to time I stopped by with baked goods for his family. He had even spoken to me once about his alcoholic brother, asking me for counsel.

"It's Christmas—yet my family is heavy in heart this season," he began. His cheery Irish cheeks gave no hint as to the weight upon his spirit. "My wife got the news that she has cancer," he said softly, not quite sure he had the courage to say those words. "She's started chemotherapy. Her weight is affected. Her hair is going. Yet she has such courage. She puts on a strong front, particularly for the children." There were six in the family.

We sat together on the front pew of the sanctuary. To our right the newly decorated church shone with bulbs and balls. To our left the baby doll representing Jesus lay quietly, peacefully. Each of the sanctuary windows had been decorated with a candle. Yet in the midst of this festive atmosphere two men's hearts sank.

"I'm so sorry to hear this," I said. "We must take this to the Lord."

We left our places, made our way to the simple altar, and knelt. Our hearts spilled before the throne of heaven. In the calm of the church a serenity began to blanket our troubled souls. It became quite easy to pray as the Spirit of a loving God drew near to bring special comfort.

I heard this man sobbing beside me, especially when I mentioned his children in prayer. I knew this would be the heaviest part of his burden.

"Lord, be near these little ones in their private worlds of anguish. In their tears, talk peace to them. In their confusion, come with heaven's understanding."

Presently the Spirit released us from our prayers. Two men stood at the front of the sanctuary just a few feet from the wooden prayer altar. We knew that, for that moment, we had done all we could do.

Richard thanked me for being a praying friend as well as a neighbor.

"When you were praying, Pastor, a special glow of the Lord settled upon my heart," he whispered. "The burden has been lifted considerably."

We walked out of the church together—one man with a healthy wife and children ready to celebrate Christmas, and the other with a sick wife and grieving children ready to attempt to celebrate. I thought back a few hours to a fallen tree with lights scattering like disobedient children across our living room carpet. We had become impatient; our day was not as perfect as we had planned.

Now I reconsidered the meaning of calamity. The tousled tree was nothing compared to a troubled neighbor. Yet in the hurt of this man I knew God was working to lift up the fallen, set aright the downcast, and bring help to the scattered children's hearts. It would take time. It would take prayer. But in the end their lives would be straightened and lightened—in one of heaven's ways or another.

# 5

# *An Inn for Christmas*

*I*'LL BRING YOU ANOTHER BLANKET."

With that, I left the church and went to my parsonage nearby. One more blanket would do it.

"Greg, when you leave in the morning, make sure you turn out the lights. I've been finding them on when I come over here in the morning. I'm trying to save on electricity. The church folk aren't rich, you know."

Greg smiled, understanding that he did have a habit of forgetting to turn out the lights in his one-room shelter at the church. He also had a habit of leaving dirty dishes in the sink downstairs in the church kitchen. Furthermore, he forgot to turn down the thermostat when going off to work each morning.

*I guess it is part of being in your early 20s,* I mused as I left this fellow.

How could parents put their child out at Christmas? That was one question that had been eating away at my heart ever since he knocked on the parsonage door.

The next day I twisted my master key into the lock, opened the door into his room, and found that he had done just as I had asked—lights off, heat turned down. But those crusty dishes were still in the sink.

*I'd better clean up this mess before the women of the church come in here to complain,* I thought.

Then I scolded myself for expecting that of the women. They knew his plight. I knew down deep inside that there would be no complaining. They, too, had sons.

"How is it that they told you to leave?" I had asked him when he wandered into my living room that desperately cold night.

"They said they had had it with my being a Christian. At first I thought they were taking to this new life of mine. But then, flip—it all turned over the other way." He had looked down at the carpet, hardly able to take it in, that his own mother and father had sent him packing.

Where else could he go? There were no relatives nearby. It was the church—that was where he would have to end up. And so there he was on my front doorstep, with his suitcase pressed against his side.

"You can use the rest rooms—shave, bathe. You can use the church kitchen to make your meals. Sometimes we'll invite you over for supper. How's that? And there's your own thermostat. It heats up just this room off the sanctuary."

I pointed out all the conveniences of being sent out in the cold at Christmas. "Of course, the sanctuary is a good place for you to go in quiet, getting your thoughts together," I suggested. Greg was a student of the Word. Since becoming a believer, he could not get enough of Scripture.

"There are some of my study books in the shelves around the corner. Take your pick. Enjoy!" I tried to be cheery, though it was not all that easy—talking to a young man who was bunking out in a side room in the church. Yes, it was the house of God. But on cold, wintry nights it was also a lonely place to walk into all by oneself. Creaks sounded in the night. Radiators croaked at odd hours.

"Just don't get caught in the rest room taking a sponge bath when someone with a key decides to case the place," I said, chuckling.

He was game. What else was left? He had finished college and had come back home to make some money to pay off some bills. And now this.

"How can parents put their own son out like that?" he asked me one especially empty evening.

"It's hard to answer that one." I shrugged, not wanting to appear too serious. I figured that if we moved on to another subject, the pain just might go away.

On the following Sunday I gently told the congregation of Greg's plight. After the worship service, people needed no prodding to get heads and hearts together. In short order, whisperings on behalf of goodwill toward the young man were filling the halls.

The Sunday before Christmas was fast approaching. We were going to enjoy our fellowship meal after the morning service.

"Do you have the box decorated?" someone asked. I assured her that Marie had everything in place—mostly hidden from Greg's view.

"Where do we put the presents?"

"Over there, behind the table. I'll get them later and put them in the box so that everything will be put together."

What fun it was to poke about, doing things in secret when it all added up to warm a heart!

"Good morning, Greg," I called out to him as he left his one-room abode to join the rest of us for Bible class.

"Good morning to you, Pastor," he replied cheerily.

Greg had been invited to his parents' for Christmas Day. He would go, he said, "to show them that I love them in spite of what they've done to me." Fine. Then go. And what would they have wrapped up under the tree for their son-put-out-of-their-home-because-of-his-faith?

The meal was eaten with relish. Such delicious tastes!

"Now?" Sally asked as she tugged at my coat.

"Now," I whispered back.

The huge box was brought out into the center of the fellowship hall.

"Greg."

It was not easy to get Greg's attention when he was eating!

"Greg, we have something special for you today. Here are some presents we have wrapped up just for you. May this be a blessed Christmas after all."

The young man—not all that tall—rose to extra height with gladness as he sauntered over to the gifts that bore his name. One by one he lifted them, poking his ear up to their sides, feeling their shapes, looking at each of us in wonder and thanksgiving.

"How can I say what's in my heart?" he asked, hardly able to say much more.

"You don't have to say anything," I responded. "Just your being with us this Christmas has made this season very special for our church family."

Christmas Day came and went.

"Greg?" I knocked on his door late Christmas night. Loud music was blaring out from inside his room. *What if someone from the church had come into the building to hear that mash called "music"?* I thought.

"Greg?" I knocked again. Presently he came to the door.

"What are you listening to?" I asked whimsically, as if not caring all that much, just making conversation.

Greg turned down the volume, then sat on the sofa made into a bed.

"I guess I was just trying to drown out something inside with that noise," Greg said haltingly.

"That bad, was it?" I ventured.

"That bad."

"And what did your parents get you for Christmas?" I asked.

"Nothing."

"Nothing? Nothing at all? Nothing? Just plain nothing?"

Greg nodded. At the other side of the room were all the gifts given by the church folk. They were now unwrapped and neatly stacked in one corner.

"My parents are not very happy people. I feel sorry for them. I'm beginning to understand that they really do need a lot of help."

I didn't know what to say.

"Their not giving me anything was really getting to me tonight. I turned up the radio so that I could drown out some of the hurt inside. I figured that no one would be here on Christmas night this late. So I thought it wouldn't harm anything—the loud music and all that."

"No problem, Greg. No one would have stopped by. I just wanted to see how you were, and that's why I decided to walk over to check things out."

"Yet, Pastor, through this whole mess I've realized one precious gift that stands out more than anything else."

"What's that?"

"It's that I *do* have a family. They are more than I have ever had in my whole life. They are all those people who come into this church. They love me. They gave me those gifts over there."

I left him and walked back home.

"How's he doing?" my wife asked as I walked through the door.

"Not too well. But not too badly either. I mean, I think this is one of the most precious Christmases Greg will ever know. For some very important reasons, this season will no doubt stand out in his memory as one of the most meaningful times in his life."

Time has passed. Greg has grown older with the rest of us. He left the church room for a second shelter and then a third as he moved from one situation to another.

Yet with the passing of the seasons, I have looked back to realize that not only for Greg but also for the entire congregation that will be one Christmastide that will highlight all the others.

It was that year all of us came to understand what it means to have been put out of an inn, only to be sheltered by the hearts of those who care enough to love.

# *6*

# *Christmas Problems*

$W$HEN WE PLACE THE NATIVITY SET UNDER THE TREE, WE dress it up and take away the pain of that first scene. But consider the problems of that first Christmas, of how bewildering it was to the people involved.

One problem was that Mary, probably a teenager, was betrothed to Joseph; however, she was pregnant, and they were not married. In those days parents decided their children should marry a certain person. This was often done without the couple involved ever having seen each other. Marriage was considered too serious to be left to the whims of youthful passions.

The betrothal period could last 12 months. It was legally binding; it could be broken only by a writ of divorce. During this time the couple was referred to as husband and wife, though they had not yet consummated their marriage.

In the 12th month the groom decided the day and hour of the ceremony, and the bride and her family were expected to be ready. How difficult it must have been for Joseph when he realized Mary was pregnant before the ceremony had taken place!

Another difficulty: Caesar Augustus had ordered a census to calculate taxes. Each male had to travel to his place of ancestry. For Joseph, this meant walking 80 miles to Bethlehem from Nazareth with Mary, who was by then "great with child." It was a difficult journey.

When the couple arrived in Bethlehem, there was no room in which to stay. The only available place was a stable in an open courtyard. Their bedding was straw, their cradle a cow's trough, and their food whatever they could muster. There Jesus was born.

Another difficulty was Herod the Great. He was king of Judea serving under Augustus, the emperor. If he suspected anyone attempting to usurp his throne, that one was eliminated. So when Herod learned that a King had been born in Bethlehem, he plotted His murder even while the competitor was but a baby.

Thus, Mary and Joseph were forced to escape to Egypt. This move southward meant gathering provisions and finding lodging and a job for Joseph. They also had to adjust to another culture. Days were bleak for the young couple.

One day an angel appeared to Joseph in a dream and told him to return to Israel with Mary and their young Child. But another problem arose. Though Herod was dead, his son Archelaus was on the throne. He, too, was bloodthirsty. Therefore, Joseph and Mary again feared for their lives. Being warned in a dream, they withdrew to the district of Galilee and settled in the town of Nazareth.

How did Joseph, Mary, and Baby Jesus make it? Angels had visited them at the times of fear and difficulty. That was the plan of God; the problems wove the providence.

In each of these problems, providence fulfilled the prophecy—

*Mary was pregnant and not married:* "Behold, a virgin shall conceive, and bear a son, and shall call his name Immanuel" (Isa. 7:14).

*The trip to Bethlehem:* "Thou, Bethlehem Ephratah, though thou be little among the thousands of Judah, yet out of thee shall he come forth unto me that is to be ruler in Israel" (Mic. 5:2).

*The threat from Herod:* "For unto us a child is born, unto us a son is given: and the government shall be upon his shoulder" (Isa. 9:6).

*The journey to Egypt:* "I . . . called my son out of Egypt" (Hos. 11:1).

*The trek back to northern Galilee's Nazareth:* "The people that walked in darkness have seen a great light: they that dwell in the land of the shadow of death, upon them hath the light shined" (Isa. 9:2).

So it is when God calls you and me. Angels visit us; then confusion sets in. We ask, "What is God doing?" We felt so close to Him last week. Now He seems to be light-years away.

At that moment we have the challenge to go with Mary and Joseph to Bethlehem. Journey with them into the night, and walk with them into the pain. This fulfills God's plan for our lives as He fulfilled His providence in their lives.

It's a matter of faith. That indeed becomes the journey. It is the trek into the unknown, believing that God is there to guide us all the way home.

# 7

# *Christmas Kindnesses*

**W**E WERE SEATED BENEATH THE MAMMOTH, LOFTY PULPIT IN Boston's historic Trinity Church. Along with some 2,000 other worshipers, we had gathered for the annual candlelight carol service.

Handsome faces wreathed in expensive scarves passed through the large, heavy curtains that divide outer quarters from the sanctuary. Women garbed in their seasonal finest gracefully seated themselves in the ancient pews.

"A person has to get here an hour early to get a seat," I overheard a fellow whisper to his friend. Even as he spoke, ushers were pointing to side walls where late arrivers could stand throughout the service.

On the expansive platform, poinsettias smothered the regal churchly furnishings. A lone gold cross hung from the front's very center, as if to crown the ornate display ablaze with color in celebration of Christ's birth.

Majestic strains pealed forth from the organ: "Trumpet Tune in C Major," by Henry Purcell; "Sonata for Flute and Organ," by George Frideric Handel; and others.

One by one, dozens of tall white candles were being lit. They stood as silent soldiers amid the flowering plants.

Our family had invited guests to join us that chilly December evening. Since this worship had become a cherished tradition to us over the years, we relished sharing it with special friends. We awaited anxiously every move, nuance, and musical offering yet to be placed before God.

Looking to my left, however, I noted a young man who did not seem to fit. He was crouched over at first, bent with his head magnetized toward the floor-boards. Then, with a sharp twist to his right, he slung himself about, rearing his black hair into the air with a jerk.

His dark eyes shot at me, then bounced away, then back again in my direction. I noticed some saliva mixing with his beard. Obviously, the well-groomed man at the other end of the pew did not notice the youth's behavior, for he was mesmerized with the lighting of the candles. I wondered what his reaction would be whenever he did glance to his left. There he would witness a crippled man with crutches, a crooked body garbed in denims and flannel shirt.

How had I missed this young man's entrance within our haloed corner of the sanctuary? Without notice, he had simply slipped in, wedging his way into our tidy mosaic of season's liturgy.

Presently I saw an usher—black-suited with a red carnation in his lapel—stoop over the young man, whispering something into his ear. "Oh no!" I gasped inwardly. After all, this *was* Christmas. And we *were* in a house of God. If ever love feasts were to be in fashion, surely this was the time. Surely that usher was not demanding that the poor young man leave for fear of disturbing the sedate!

The usher left him. His head flipped back again while two hands led two arms into jutted motions scraping the air. One leg shot out and then back against the floor. His eyes darted back to me. Fright was all over his face.

All of a sudden I felt sick, not because of this poor creature, but because of my own fear of what was going to happen to him. Torture is commonplace, and violence has been with us since the first two sons scuffled in the field. But surely we would not have to live down a mean display of pretense at Christmas.

People kept milling about, some stretching their necks, hoping they would find some tiny space on a pew for sitting. Few caught sight of the intense drama going on nearby. What could I do? I had no authority in this church. There was no speedy network of rescue that I could call into play and relieve the anxious, confused black eyes beneath his furrowed brow.

Seemingly out of nowhere, an attractive young lady seated herself beside this youth. I saw her place her hand upon his shoulder, then lean near to his ear, whispering something. Her smile was comforting, understanding, as she turned her head to look straight into his eyes. Presently those distraught limbs began to calm down, and his head settled itself more evenly atop his neck.

*What are they going to do with him?* I thought. *Will they, even with a veneer of kindness, lead him away from the rest of us? What game will they play to convince him that he would enjoy the service better from a side room somewhere?*

She said no more. She just sat there, listening to Vierne's "Westminster Carillon" from the organ.

The usher who had spoken with the young man then passed right in front of him, going across the aisle to the second pew from the front. That tall churchman had spotted a space 12 inches wide. With diplomatic graciousness, the usher informed the person seated next to that space that he would have a visitor sharing the worship.

Back to the attractive lady and crippled man the usher made his way. Gently, he lifted the young man under his arm, taking the crutches in his other hand. It was as if the Red Sea parted there for the crossing of this twosome; no one interfered. In no time, the youth discovered himself being presented with the best seat in the house. Smilingly, the person to his right welcomed the lad into the pew.

Again, seemingly out of nowhere, a man in his late 20s—dressed in denims and flannel shirt, his hair tied in a knot at the back of head—knelt down alongside the crippled one. I watched him assist the other in shedding his winter jacket, first one arm and then the other drawn out of the sleeves. Next, he carefully placed the crutches on the floor right inside the seat. That done, the kind man joined the attractive lady elsewhere, but within eyeshot of the crippled man.

It was then that I heard the opening Christmas hymn being sung from a far back balcony. The soprano lifted her voice with

> *Once in royal David's city*
> *Stood a lowly cattle shed,*
> *Where a mother laid her Baby*
> *In a manger for His bed . . .*

I could not help but turn around to see the sight. There was the robed soloist surrounded by others dressed in holy day splendor. After all, this was the start of something very special. Worship had begun.

Slowly I turned back to face the sanctuary's front. But in the turning I glanced again at "my friend." I saw then the most marvelous sight. Still mixed with the hairs of his black beard was a bit of spittle, but now in his eyes I saw joy. He, too, had heard the opening words of Christmas praise. He was looking over at the attractive lady and her companion. I did not mean to be prying, but I could not help but glance at them as well. There they were, beaming with kindnesses rendered, so happy that he was all right, that he had been given a good place to sit, so ready for the worship of the King.

On the second verse, the congregation was to join the soloist. With a shining face, the youth twisted his mouth in jubilation. The furrow was gone from his forehead, thank God. And with the rest of us he was singing forth—

*With the poor and mean and lowly*
*Lived on earth our Savior holy.*

Although it was still days before the 25th, I knew in my heart that for me, at least, Christmas had begun.

# *The Simple Gifts of Christmas*

$T$HE CAR CLOCK READ 3:51 P.M. WE PULLED OUT OF OUR driveway and headed north for a small village tucked into central Nova Scotia. My wife and I buckled ourselves into the front seat while our two youngsters cozied themselves in the back.

It was Christmas Eve, and we were on our way to Grandma's. That meant mince pie, filled cookies, a freshly cut tree from the backwoods, and lots of chatter. It also meant we had a 12-hour ride ahead of us.

On, Prancer! On, Vixen!

Jay and Heidi Jo had opened two brightly colored, fluffy puppets in the shapes of parrots—the first of their Christmas presents. "They'll help keep them occupied on the trip," my wife had said.

Why is it that when a lunch is packed for a jaunt, it's only a few minutes into the trip before the gastric juices start churning, even when it's not mealtime? The freshly made sandwiches looked like gourmet delights as we headed up the interstate. "Anybody for an apple? An orange? How about a Twinkie instead?" Forget rules of nutrition on holidays!

I knew better than to flip on the cassette of Handel's "Allegro Maestoso" from *Water Music* when the other three passengers were clamoring for "The Twelve Days of Christmas." I also knew that "I'll Be Home for Christmas," "Here We Come A-Caroling," and other favorites would follow. Handel would have to wait until after midnight.

How did we manage to squeeze everything into the trunk?

"I didn't wrap the gifts," my wife informed me. "I figured that, crossing the border into Canada, the last thing we needed was for all those presents to go under inspection. I brought along some gift wrap and bows for decorating the presents after we get there." Such is the intrigue of going to another country!

Soon the winter day became dusky and then dark. With the oncoming night, lights twinkled from households throughout Maine. Towns came alive with reds, blues, oranges, whites, and greens. Reindeer pranced over lawns. Nativity scenes shone from front yards. Angels sang from rooftops. Bushes in front of houses bounced their colored lights in the brisk winds. Shopping centers outdid themselves in splendor.

Even the turnpike tollbooths were wreathed and bowed. Those handling the change called out, "Merry Christmas!"—their rosy cheeks beaming against the cold. Overhead signs read PORTLAND, BRUNSWICK, BELFAST, BANGOR.

Eventually, the elated, chirpy chimings of the four of us were spaced with silences until I noted in the rearview mirror that two little heads had their eyes closed. The parrot puppets seemed to have nodded off as well. Then the passenger to my right gave in too, her head resting on a pillow propped against the side window.

Did I dare slip in Handel yet?

On into the night we sped northward, passing over the border without incident. On either side of the road, fields glistened with snow. Farmhouses packed over the hills, their barns stoically silhouetted against the star-scattered sky.

Hour upon hour the three slept. Hour after hour the carols poured from the car radio. Melodies in country-western rhythm, cathedral chants, choral arrangements, and orchestral fantasies filled all the spaces with wonder.

Even past midnight I noticed that houses were well lit, lawns bathed in color. No window blinds were drawn; instead, I could see family members celebrating inside their warm, secure walls.

"Are you getting tired?" my wife mumbled occasionally as she shifted her position slightly, only to doze off again when assured that I was wide awake. I could hardly believe it myself. The later it grew, the more awake I became. Was it the stirring of some Christmas tonic? If so, I had no intentions of squelching it.

One o'clock. Two o'clock. Then three o'clock in the morning, and I was still wide-eyed. The house lights still beamed bright and beautiful, and the stream of Christmas music (even some of Handel's works, to my delight) kept flowing from every radio station on the dial. Overhead the heavens peeped through with lanterns in the shivering breezes, while meadows stood as patient props in the grandest drama of the year.

*This is Christmas!* I said to myself, overcome with joy. *What beautiful gifts God has given me!—a journey, a loving family, welcoming lights, the crowned outdoors, music, and His adventure.*

These gifts, no doubt, were similar to what another family had experienced long ago. The young couple with baby-to-be were presented as well with a jaunt, one another, Bethlehem's star, Israel's rocky and enticing landscape, an angelic cantata, and the Father's overshadowing.

How extravagant of the Lord to put all this in place for His own—yet how simple for us who receive! All that's needed is eyes with which to behold it, a heart with which to cherish it, and a spirit with which to give thanks.

# *9*

# *Christmas All Year Through*

$W$HEN OUR DENOMINATIONAL COMPASSIONATE MINISTRIES office came out with a calendar through which to aid the world's hungry and destitute, our congregation caught on to the idea with enthusiasm. Such a novel approach for both children and adults!

Each Sunday we collected the people's special in-gatherings with which to lift the globe's poor. It was particularly enriching during the holiday gift-giving month, because we knew that while we presented wrapped-up gifts to friends and relatives here at home, we were also presenting our money gifts to world missions.

At the front of the sanctuary under the Christmas tree we placed a large box, complete with its own seasonal wrappings and striking red bow. Across the bow's front was taped a gift tag reading "COMPASSIONATE MINISTRIES." Little tots strained to reach the top of the box, dumping their coins inside, while the older folks gave their bills and personal checks. As we stood there singing a missionary hymn, we were reminded that the Bethlehem Babe came not only for that hamlet neighboring Jerusalem but also for the whole world. God so loved that He gave. (See John 3:16.)

After the holidays, the sanctuary decorations were dismantled, packed again in their neatly stacked boxes, and readied for yet another season. But we simply could not throw away that compassionate ministries box. It was still too attractive in its own dressing. Some had asked that it be made available for still one more Sunday. Most importantly, we knew that the hungry people of the world did not simply "wrap up" and go away at the end of December. Their lined, stark faces covered with flies, their lean, bone-showing bodies, their death-drawn eyes still stared out at us in our opulent culture.

Could we nonchalantly go back to our gorging, our moneygrubbing, pushing out the barn walls with still more toys to bounce, wind up, and throw away? No. We would have to keep in front of us those fellow human beings who were languishing about the face of the planet. As followers of the One who came to heal, lift, and comfort, we had to continue to do what we could do in carrying out His mission.

So even after the first Sunday of the new year, collecting from those who had forgotten their givings with the holiday rush, the box stayed at the front of the sanctuary. Now it was no longer under the tree, but atop the Communion table in plain view of all.

It is our plan to keep the box in view throughout the year. So it will not become too familiar, we hide it away for a Sunday or two and then bring it out during the Sunday morning worship service to ask for moneys from those who simply feel led to give "some more"—spur-of-the-moment, spontaneous offerings received without a lot of preparation or prodding.

We pray our Christmas box will not only continue to augment the fund but also enlarge our vision of a starving world. Our desire is to pray for them earnestly, more consistently. How exciting it is for us to celebrate this joyous sacrifice—not for just one month, but all year through!

# My "Nice Guy" Christmas

*I* WAS IN A HURRY DRIVING INTO THE MALL PARKING LOT, hardly looking to the right or left.

"Slow down!" the right side of my brain instructed the left side. It was somewhere in that midconscious level that thoughts were targeting one another for reason.

How many errands were buzzing in my tired head!

Somewhere in my peripheral vision there was a young girl pushing a load of shopping carts toward the grocery store. There must have been 20 to 30 of those huge metal carriers locked into one another.

I had space enough. There was no danger. I could swing around that slow-moving train of silver gleam headed for the lineup outside the food mart.

So I meandered my car to the right of the carriages, then spied an empty space near the drugstore where I could park and dash in for a quick purchase.

As I flung open the car door, I looked up to see the young girl. She was peering straight at me. How could she have gotten to that part of the parking lot so quickly after having pushed all those heavy carts? Anyway, there she was, a hurt look on her face.

"When are you going to learn to drive with sense?" she called out to me, not very happy with my presence.

With a sad glance down to the pavement, she

turned around, having accomplished what her sense of justice had prodded. Before I realized what had happened, she had disappeared among the cars that were lined up like toy soldiers.

I went into the drugstore, bought my trinket, and felt troubled way down inside. All of a sudden the Christmas cheer had disappeared from my heart. No amount of painted reindeer on poles outside could erase the picture of that girl's look.

*What have I done?* I asked my wilted inner self.

What I had done was drive thoughtlessly, carelessly. I had also brought pain to a young person at the most holy season of the year. It simply was not right.

But what could I do about it? She was gone, meshed in with the hubbub outside. She'd be forgotten in the day's upset.

However, when I walked toward my car again, there she was. But this time she was not bothering to scold me. She was simply gathering another heap of carriages, tugging at their arms and legs to get them in line for another trip back to the stone wall.

I saw her face again. It was not happy. She was cold, tired, and wanting to go home after a long day.

I lifted the door latch to get inside, where it was warm. But I couldn't lift my legs into the car. I had to shut the door and walk over to that girl's side.

As I approached her, I thought that she might become scared, thinking I was going to confront her. So I put out my hand toward hers, starting to talk even before I was close to her.

"I am so sorry," I started. "I want you to know that I am really sorry," I repeated, just in case she didn't pick up my first words. "I want to apologize to you for what I did. You see, I was driving but not thinking about what I was doing. I saw you, but I didn't see you. I saw those carts you were pushing, but I guess it just didn't register all that precisely in my head what was going on. Have you ever had that happen to you?"

She looked up at me, wondering what was going on. Was I playing games with her, or was I sincere?

"You see, I'm really a nice guy. I don't enjoy being rude to people. But I was impolite to you today. I hurt you—and that hurt me. So I just want you to know that I didn't mean what I did, and I ask for your forgiveness."

She broke into the broadest smile, then reached out her hand to shake mine. A sigh came from her lips, relieved to know that I was not going to add insult to injury. I really was trying to make things right, she reasoned.

"Yes, I do know what you're talking about. I've had days like that too." She laughed as one human understanding another. "You know, you really are a nice guy. Thanks a lot. Thanks. Thanks an awful lot."

I turned and walked back to the car, opened the door, climbed inside, and drove away. As I passed by her and the shopping carts, she lifted a hand to wave good-bye. I waved back, glad that I had retrieved the nice guy inside. In doing that, I had made two people happy.

I had also brought back the cheer of reindeer painted on poles all around me. It was that good feeling that comes especially at Christmastime.

*11*

# *Christmas Simplicity*

$L$UKE 2:1-20.

*"And it came to pass . . ."* (v. 1, NKJV).

Imagine the nonchalance of the record. The account at the beginning of Luke 2 is about to tell us of the Incarnation—the coming of Deity into human form. Yet it starts the story with nothing other than one syllable words: "And it came to pass."

So it is frequently in our own lives. What God does with us for eternity's sake is often stepped out in silence or mere muffles, with not much fanfare. It is the simplicity of His doings that astounds us, particularly when we are so taken up with the grand and opulent.

We are absorbed with sorting out the minors from the majors in our biographies. We want more majors and fewer minors. We want our lives to be significant, to count for something marvelous. Yet how often has God done something profound in our days by understatement—the minors? It is only later that we discover that, from eternity's viewpoint, the minor was indeed a major. "And it came to pass."

Therefore, it behooves us simply to trust and obey, to leave the details of importance with God and so live for today's opportunities of nonchalance.

*"That a decree went out from Caesar Augustus . . ."* (v. 1, NKJV).

Once again we are dumbfounded with this telling.

The record providing specifics concerning the coming of the Messiah starts not with religion but with politics. It details not what God is up to but what government is up to. The focus is not on the Holy Spirit but on Caesar Augustus.

So it is with much of our lives as well. What God does for us and with us is frequently wrapped up in the world's doings. Take, for instance, the life of Corrie ten Boom. She and her family housed Jews who were being hunted by Nazis. They befriended these frightened people in the name of Jesus, saving them from certain death. We are inspired by what the ten Booms did for God because of the government's action against their lives. Likewise, Caesar's power plays squeezed out the Spirit's witness.

The same can be said for Dietrich Bonhoeffer, a German pastor-professor who stood up to Adolf Hitler. For his Christian stand he was put in prison and then hung in Eastertide 1943. We are enriched by his life and writings because of the way politics evoked courage from his soul.

We can look back upon many dedicated lives to conclude that God's work is frequently understood long after. Then we also realize that while Caesar passes on, God remains, as does His holy venture.

*"This census first took place . . ."* (v. 2, NKJV).

More political details. The recorder tells us simply that there was a counting of heads—names listed on a register. Yet we understand that at work beneath this counting of heads is God's counting of souls.

For instance, God knows He can count on the commitments of a Mary and Joseph as well as some magi and scrubby shepherds. On the flip side, He cannot count on Herod or those Roman soldiers, and some years hence He will not be able to count on the help of one named Pontius Pilate.

Therefore, we are reminded in the Christmas story

of the Great Count—the Judgment Day that is not only at the close of our lives but every day. When God registers our doings, what do they add up to? Can we be numbered with the Marys and Josephs or with the Herods?

*"All went to be registered, everyone to his own city"* (v. 3, NKJV).

Still we are not getting very far into the obvious pronouncements of divinity. We are yet provided background concerning the decrees of government. However, beneath that the designings of God are certainly at work. Could Caesar ever have realized that his dictum was in fact providing for the fulfillment of Old Testament predictions? Would he ever know that his press upon the populace also forced a young couple out of Nazareth into Bethlehem for the seeing-through of prophetic detail?

In God's simplicity, His nonchalance, He works through history's events to accomplish His plans. His hand is not always detectable on the surface, at first glance. Later, though, His intervention becomes evident.

In our own lives, then, we are to keep the faith midst all sorts of worldly happenings. We are to live by Rom. 8:28: "All things work together for good to those who love God, to those who are the called according to His purpose" (NKJV).

When we are willed into the divine will, we then see that what life does *with* us is what God is doing *for* us. The Bible is filled with real-life examples of this trusting principle. There is Joseph in the Old Testament, who went from the pit to the prison to the palace. God was in it. Daniel went from the lions' den to become Deity's spokesman to a needy culture. God was in it. Jesus was strung upon Calvary's tree in order to rise again. God was in it.

*"Joseph also went up from Galilee, out of the city of Nazareth"* (v. 4, NKJV).

As God leads us along, we never know what a

journey may yield. Certainly when Joseph became burdened with the task of the trek 80 miles southward to Bethlehem—packing clothing, food, closing his carpenter's shop, caring for pregnant Mary—he did not know how mightily God was at work in the tether.

It is the same with our Christian lives. We meet someone along the way, and our entire lives are changed. We read something, and our thoughts are never the same. We go to an appointment, and from that time onward we take a different road. We travel to a particular city and find new dimensions we had never known before. We attend a particular college or university and meet someone who transforms our futures.

Chuck Colson was sent to prison for crimes committed during the Watergate scandal. While there behind bars, he met believers who told him about Jesus. His life has never been the same.

Did Joseph ever dream that in his going from Nazareth to Bethlehem his life would be embedded into religious history forever—for good?

*"To be registered with Mary . . ."* (v. 5, NKJV).

When we make our journeys in life, it is not pleasant to go it alone. On your way to Bethlehem, take someone with you.

Thank God that we are not called to a monastic walk nor a recluse religion. Hebrews 12:1 reminds us that we are surrounded by a cloud of witnesses. It is a community of faith we belong to. We are a part of the best crowd ever.

No wonder Jesus enjoyed the company of His disciples. When John met Him, brother James joined in too. When Andrew discovered the Lord, he ran to tell his brother Peter. How heartening to read of a household—Mary, Martha, Lazarus—who lived under mercy! And when Zacchaeus came to grace, he took the whole village to his heart.

Is there someone—spouse, child, parent, friend—

who will believe with you on your way to Bethlehem? Who will get hold of the simplicity of Christmas?

*"The days were completed ..."* (v. 6, NKJV).

Once again we are offered the gift of time as we are given it in verse 1: "And it came to pass . . ." (NKJV).

God works in time—so don't hurry Him. And what He starts, He completes. It's so with each segment of your life as well. Trust the love of His vision.

We are so concerned with our calendars—minutes, hours, days, weeks, months, years. God is more concerned with our characters—values, reputations, influences, positionings of the heart.

Keep in mind that it does take time to birth a baby. It also takes time to birth one into grace, obedience, and a life of holiness. The maturation process is God's gift, His way.

We would hurry. God would hover. We would push. God would prepare. Remind yourself of the scriptural phrase "when the fullness of time had come" (Gal. 4:4, NKJV).

*"She brought forth her firstborn Son"* (v. 7, NKJV).

So it was that in the midst of the pain, there was the pleasure. Can you see it, too, in your own life? The spoiled pout; the saved of the Kingdom do not pout, but praise Him—even in the pain.

Mary and Joseph were so alone; yet at the same time they were awakened by the face of newborn Jesus. They were terribly confused; but just the same, they were comforted by His tender presence. They were poor; yet they were plenteous with the birth of their firstborn. They were tired; but their countenances shone with triumph when looking into the boy's face. They were bushed; yet they were blessed.

This truth is there for us if we can but see it with the eyes of faith. In simplicity we know the pleasure of His presence in the midst of pain.

*"She . . . wrapped Him in swaddling cloths, and laid Him in a manger"* (v. 7, NKJV).

"Make do," they say. Mary knew how to "make do." There was no comfortable room for Mary and Joseph in the inn; so they made do in the stable.

We can live with simplicity, trusting Jesus to teach us how to make do. We are handed nothing more than a manger. "Fine," we say, "as long as it is with Jesus." We are given nothing more than a stable. "OK," we reply, "with Jesus." There is nothing but cows for friends. "Great, as long as God blesses," we say.

What is it that God has given you with which to "make do"? Is it a smile to share, a note to send, a prayer to offer, a phone call to make, a compliment to give?

*". . . no room for them in the inn"* (v. 7, NKJV).

We are troubled many times because we cannot see the hand of God obviously in our lives. Do we not understand that God delights in disguises, in the maskings?

When there is no room in the inn, He puts us in the stable. Can we take it? Can we live up to it? Can we discover the adventure in it? God can work His will in the zigzag.

Learn then from the old, old story of love. Take the journey once more to Bethlehem. Be up and going. Make do with what God has provided. Pray for the eyes with which to see the invisible. Go forth with the merry heart and seek holy adventures with the faith-filled soul. In so doing, you will come upon the manger. And there you will discover yourself bent over, bowing in the glow of the One who has come not only to save our souls but also to show us the way of gladness.

# 12

# *New Spirit of Christmas*

$O$K, I'VE HAD IT.

Last year I waited for the Christmas music, spun the dial around, stayed up late to see if some disc jockey would dare sneak it in after midnight. But, no. The Christmas songs began to air only a scant few hours before Christmas Day.

*So now finally I can bask in the music for which the season was meant,* I sighed. I thought that at least till midnight on Christmas Day I would hear the melodies meant for December. But by midevening the carols began to fade out. So much for years past, when Christmas music filled our hearts all month long.

When I went to buy Christmas cards, I looked for greetings marked "religious," and my selection was limited to but a few. Santa and "Season's Greetings" filled the racks; there was little offered about Jesus.

"Religious cards," I asked the clerk. "Where are they? It's Christmas. The birth of Jesus. I can hardly find any cards about that. Don't you have any?"

She looked at me as though she had just stumbled across an alien, shrugged her shoulders, and disappeared.

Meandering through stores in search of a fresh Nativity scene to place under our Christmas tree, I came upon plenty of New England village scenes, Santa seated in overstuffed chairs, Santa dangling packs filled with toys, Santa patting little children's heads, but nowhere a Nativity scene.

When I did finally stumble upon one, it was so motley that no one would want it. Besides, it was stashed so far up on the shelves that it was practically impossible to retrieve.

Malls were packed with the revelers in search of presents. There were plenty of scenes depicting old St. Nick—now deified to replace the Babe. Children scampered all over one another to get their pictures taken with the jolly fellow.

The political mandate of separation of church and state has finally soaked to the grass roots. But this is ridiculous. Will we have to live through many more Christmases like this? If so, it won't be long until Christmas truly will have its own natural replacement—the "winter holiday."

I recall another nation on the planet that tried that. Right from the Bolshevik Revolution it seemed to work—until all of a sudden the celebration stopped, the festive flags stopped waving, and the whole wretched castle came tumbling down. The Soviet Union and its atheistic satellite countries fell. Communism had done itself in.

If this is the route *we* have chosen, why take so long to get there? Let's just throw out everything that truly has to do with the historical basis of Christmas: Jesus, Mary, Joseph, the manger, and all the rest. Who needs them? Obviously this country doesn't.

It's time that somebody climbed to the top of the heap and demanded that we do this thing right. Perhaps the American Civil Liberties Union would volunteer to appoint a chairperson to see this revolution through.

Any takers?

# Senior Ornaments on Our Tree

*I*'M GOING INTO THE HOSPITAL. THEN THEY'LL LET ME OUT TO come back home to die!"

Everett was 94 years old. He had to go to the hospital—doctor's orders. After that, back to his senior apartment to die—at least so he concluded with a gesture of his huge arm.

Yet this was Christmas. And we at the church could not permit this Christian gentleman such a mood at Christmas. Younger participants in the church's Senior Adult Ministry (SAM) had suggested we cheer up those older ones by surprising them on a December Saturday morning.

"Let's package up our favorite cookies for those folks," one of the women suggested. "We'll deliver them to their homes, sing some carols, then wish them God's best."

No sooner said than done.

One of those Maine winter snows had settled upon the ground as SAM enthusiasts gathered in front of the country church. In hand were decorated gift boxes filled with delicious morsels. Inside our hearts were carols ready to be sung to our friends.

So it was that Everett greeted us, at first not able to make out who we were because of his poor eyesight. Yet in short order each of us grasped his hands, leaned into his vision, and extended warm Christmas greetings.

"Come again," he cheerfully waved toward us as we left him with a prayer. It is more blessed to give than to receive, we concluded when leaving his residence.

Then on to see Alice. She met us at her front door as she was about to put more birdseed into the feeder outside her kitchen window.

"I wasn't expecting you!" she exclaimed.

"That's right," we answered. "Just the way we wanted it." We filled her house with Christmas cheer.

Winding up Douglas Mountain to see Loann and Gertrude took more time than we had expected. They lived nearly an hour from the church. With winter ice, this was sometimes extra-adventurous traveling for them. Yet they were faithful to worship on the Lord's Day.

Knocking on their front door brought no response. But I could hear them inside the cozy country house. They were simply tucked away at the far end of the place.

Wading through the snow to a side window, I rapped on the pane. There was Loann, who jolted around to stare at me. She had been on the phone, standing alongside their newly decorated tree.

"Just a moment," she motioned to me.

In a minute or two we were all shaking hands, exchanging best wishes, and sharing their usual humor inside their welcoming abode. A huge fire roared in the fireplace.

"How nice of you to stop in this morning!" Loann's mother said as we prepared to leave. Here were two church women—mother and daughter— who made *our* Saturday more Christmaslike. They always did that. A person always departed their presence with more joy in the heart than when entering. It was their gift to their friends.

On to Ruth's senior apartment. We just had to see the community room, she insisted. There in the corner was the gorgeous Christmas tree that once stood in *her* living room back at her house in a neighboring village.

"I'm so glad I could donate that to the others, this being my first Christmas away from that house I lived in for more than 30 years. I feel so good to know that my tree has come with me. And now others enjoy it too."

She took us on a welcomed tour of the place—up and down the halls to see the door decorations. "Some of my friends have outdone themselves!" she exclaimed with pride.

And on and on we went. How that morning flew!

"This has been the real start to my Christmas," one of the travelers remarked as we drove back into the church parking lot. "I would not have missed this for anything."

The reason? Because we had visited the wonder-filled senior ornaments on our church's friendship tree.

# All I Want for Christmas Is a Day by Myself

*I*T'S CHRISTMAS, AND I HAVE CONCLUDED THAT AT THE RISK of playing Mr. Scrooge, I must make a plea for some time by myself.

You see, thus far this December I have battled with clerks, elevator crews, service station attendants (while being honked at from behind), and wrapping paper that wants to crinkle in the wrong places.

I have also done my share of mopping the church basement of water that has seeped in around the walls because of the melting of the snow from last week's blizzard. I have propped up the sanctuary tree for the umpteenth time, praying solemnly that it will not make its final fall until after New Year's. In addition, I have just realized that I should have ordered another case of white candles for the watch night service. I was banking on the old ones being long enough; however, to my horror this morning I found nothing but stubs in the rectangular box on the storage closet shelf. Not only that, but also I discovered clots in the grape juice for Communion.

At the start of this brand-new, snow-laden day— just a week from Christmas—my discerning wife sensed that this needed to be *my* day. Even before breakfast was served, she nudged her way toward me and said, "I think the children and I will go shopping today and leave you alone."

There were no howls of protest. I did not gather up my picket signs. I simply laid myself limp into her remark and, with doelike eyes catching her glance, I smiled. We made connection, and it was grand. She knew that what I needed, more than anything else this Christmas, was one day by myself.

Since they left I have pinched myself to see if in fact I have not died and gone to heaven. Would you believe that for one solid hour I've listened to the kind of music *I* want to hear? I have drunk a cup of tea, actually knowing what it was that I put past my lips. I have even read completely through this morning's newspaper without once being interrupted to tie a shoe, put on a boot, find a mitten, or wipe a nose.

To celebrate this moment of simplicity, I have turned on the Christmas tree lights (only to find that one string has gone out) and made myself a peanut-butter-and-jelly sandwich. (Oh, you can forget the peanut butter—there was none, but I used my imagination and made the best of it—after all, it's Christmas.)

The only other person I have permitted audience with my soul has been the mailman. Along with the bright cards, he brought me bills from Sears, Texaco, and Montgomery Ward. Yet I will not allow them to ruin my day, so I have tucked them under the TOMORROW clip that rests atop the refrigerator. Perhaps they will get lost in the penuche.

There are sugar cookies on the kitchen counter, freshly made by my teenage daughter. There are lemon drops and date squares. Gingerbread boys and girls dance across the table. Why is it that a fallen world has such enticing delicacies to tempt the preacher who already tips 10 more pounds on the scales than he ought? Even though it's holiday time, I will refrain.

The hours have passed, and I have relaxed for the first time in weeks. I still have yet to break into *No For-*

*eign Land,* the biography of a Native American. But it has been fun. And the door opening wide to let in my family does good things to my spirit.

To prove my gratitude to her, I have slipped an envelope under her dinner plate. To the strains of "Deck the Halls," she will open it after tonight's tofu and there read: "Thank you for some time to myself. It was a most thoughtful Christmas present. Now for New Year's, I give you YOUR day too. Take it when you wish. Love."

Merry Christmas, one and all!